THE COMPLETE
WEDDING
SPEECH
GUIDE

THE COMPLETE
WEDDING
SPEECH
GUIDE

ANDREW BYRNE

NEW
HOLLAND

808.3Y/C

This revised edition published in 2011 by New Holland Publishers (UK) Ltd

First published in the UK in 2004 by
New Holland Publishers (UK) Ltd
London • Auckland • Sydney • Cape Town

Garfield House, 86–88 Edgware Road, London W2 2EA United Kingdom
80 McKenzie Street, Cape Town 8001 South Africa
Unit 1, 66 Gibbes Street, Chatswood, NSW 2067, Australia
218 Lake Road, Northcote, Auckland, New Zealand

A catalogue record for this book is available from the British Library.

ISBN 978 1 84773 924 7

Publisher: Aruna Vasudevan
Senior Editor: Charlotte Macey
Cover Design: Vanessa Green, The Urban Ant Ltd.
Inside Design: Sally Bond
Production: Sarah Kulasek

Reproduction by Pica Digital Pte. Ltd, Singapore
Printed and bound in India by Replika Press

2 4 6 8 10 9 7 5 3 1

Contents

Introduction

It's a common misconception that delivering a wedding speech, especially your first, is similar to leaping from an aeroplane with an umbrella for a parachute. The fact is, writing and giving a speech doesn't have to be like that at all.

There are two golden rules for delivering a well-received speech and actually enjoying the moment – preparation and practice. In clear, straightforward steps this book will guide you through planning, writing, and delivering your speech on 'the big day'. Whether you are the bride, groom, father of the bride, best man, friend, relative, Master of Ceremonies or even a last-minute speaker, this guide is intended to help you deliver the best possible speech .

'Speech contents' (pages 9–49) and 'Planning and writing the speech' (pages 51–77) will take you through the speech writing process: discovering what a person in your role normally says; deciding what you want to say; using a speech outline; practical writing tips; humour 'do's and don'ts' and writing and rehearsing the speech (using tested techniques).

Finally, in 'Delivering your speech' (pages 79–92) all the secret ingredients for confidently and enjoyably delivering your speech on the day are revealed. This part of the book also takes you through warming-up, curing stage fright and projecting confidence in your voice.

Aided by techniques used in public speaking and by research and experience, this guide will help to ensure that you and your speech are ready for the wedding day.

Your speech is an opportunity to tell loved ones how you feel about them on the most celebrated day in a couple's life. It's an honour and a privilege and should also be a pleasure. Allow yourself to enjoy that moment!

– Andrew Byrne

Speech contents

Although speeches and their contents can vary greatly,
the advice given in the following pages explains what a person
in your role would be expected to say.

Don't be afraid to break with tradition if you want to,
but do make sure you thank the right people and offer
a toast to the married couple.

Master of Ceremonies

Most weddings have some form of Master of Ceremonies (MC) acting as circus ringmaster. The MC can either be a close friend or relative, the best man or even a professional MC. In some cases the married couple may even ask the father of the bride – it's their choice of course.

Besides speaking, the MC generally also ensures that the reception location is ready before the guests arrive. The MC acts as the reception's greeter. When it is time for the speeches, the MC gets the attention of the guests by calling for silence. From then on, the MC's role is to introduce each speaker, as arranged. Some couples prefer to have a toast-master, rather than an MC; he or she simply calls for silence and introduces the speakers.

Who is the MC?

The best man

If the role of MC is being filled by the best man, he will be the first and last person to speak, with his best man's speech coming at the very end. Other than that, he should fulfil the MC's tasks below.

A professional MC

Nowadays, you can hire a professional MC to organize and manage the speakers at your wedding, with the benefit that the MC is experienced – he or she knows how to perk up the crowd and keep the speeches flowing, preventing any flat spots between speakers. However, some couples find the idea of using a stranger to speak at their wedding disconcerting or odd – it's all a matter of choice. If you decide to go for a professional MC, you should shop around and keep the following tips in mind:

- If possible, use an MC who has been recommended by someone you trust.
- Interview the prospective MC and make sure you feel comfortable with him or her.
- Ask for references from previous clients.

A professional MC should be:

- Confident, but not cocky.
- Able to listen to your requirements and not dictate them.
- Courteous and considerate.

Preparation

Unlike the other speakers, the MC's speech is structured around the entire series of speeches. So, unless you're also delivering your own speech (such as the best man) you won't have to delve into stories about how the groom locked himself out of his car and then got arrested for trying to break into it. Of course, if such a story is a great link to introducing the next speaker (such as the policeman who arrested him) then go ahead and use it.

While you should stick to the speech writing rules in 'Planning and writing the speech', pages 51–77, you have more of an opportunity to speak from the top of your head, as your main job is to introduce the next, and thank the previous, speaker.

MC's organizational tasks

Although this is outside the area of speech writing, it is helpful to be aware of the other roles the MC traditionally performs. Depending on how the reception is organized by the wedding couple, the MC may also be called upon to ensure the reception location is ready for when the guests arrive. The MC's role may include:

- Making sure the tables (including place names) are set as planned.
- Officially welcoming guests and formally announcing the guests' names to the wedding couple and party if there is a receiving line.
- Ensuring the meal is punctual and drinks are flowing as per the wishes of the bride and groom.
- Managing the sequence of speeches (explained below).
- Organizing the cutting of the wedding cake.
- Organizing the first dance (if required).
- Gathering the guests for the throwing of the bride's bouquet prior to the departure of the bridal couple.
- Gathering the guests together at the end of the reception to bid farewell to the couple.
- Helping to arrange the packing up of items such as flowers and the wedding cake.

MC's speech tasks

It's the MC's job to set a positive tone for the evening and the speeches to follow. As with speeches in general, if you are relaxed and enjoying yourself, the audience will pick up on this. That's half of your job done already.

Before the meal

- Welcome the guests at the door, introduce yourself and tell them that you will be their MC.
- Formally welcome the guests once they are seated and thank them for coming.
- If there are any additional features to the reception (such as games) explain them – keep the explanation clear and straightforward.

When the bridal party enters

- Officially introduce the bridal party to the guests and allow them to take their seats at the top table.
- Comment on the great day so far and make the guests feel involved by asking if they're having a good time.
- Thank the bride and groom for asking you to be their MC.

Post-meal speeches

When the meal is finished, it's time for the MC to get the attention of the guests. Conversations around the tables will be in full swing by now. If the reception is large and noisy then bring your glass to the microphone. Tapping a glass for attention is not just tradition – it works. Once heads start to turn and voices lower, it's time to speak. The nearest tables will settle down first and the rest should follow.

The guests have eaten and should be feeling content and ready for the speeches. This is a crucial part in the speeches sequence. Like a warm-up act, you are setting the mood for the speakers to follow.

- Call for silence, for example, 'Ladies and gentlemen, if I could have your attention for a moment please…', perhaps adding that you hope they're well fed and happy.
- Once you have their attention you'll find there's still energy in the room from the crowd's conversations. You have about half a minute to make the most of that 'energy' after they fall quiet.
- Introduce the first speaker. When they've finished and have sat down, you step up, thank that speaker and introduce the next person, and so on and so forth.
- If the wedding couple are happy for any cards or emails to be read out by you, do this after the main speakers have finished – if the MC is also the best man, he should read them out during his speech.

- Again, if you are the MC and the best man, your speech should come at the very end (see pages 32–35).
- If you are not giving a speech, end by thanking everyone once more and wishing them a wonderful time – you could even end by proposing a final toast.

After the speeches

- With the speeches finished, announce the cutting of the cake (depending on the wedding couple's plans).
- If there is dancing, this is followed by announcing the first dance – invite the newlyweds to take to the dance floor.
- After the wedding couple have had a chance to enjoy being alone on the dance floor (although some find it awkward), invite the rest of the wedding party to join them and shortly afterwards extend this invitation to the rest of the guests.

Time to go

- Assemble the guests and let them know the bride is ready to throw her bouquet (if she has decided to do so).
- When the couple are ready to leave, make sure the guests are assembled, and announce the departure of the bridal couple.

Advice

Try to gauge the mood of the guests. If you feel their attention may be slipping, try to pick up the pace and get them charged up again. One way of helping this (and increasing table activity) is to include some form of a game in the proceedings.

Pit each table against the others. One idea is to ask them to write the most amazing toast from the guests to the bride and groom. Asking each table to write a poem about the newlyweds is also a good technique. Even better is asking them to write it in the form of a limerick, which always results in hilarity. It encourages people to think up the most amusing lines and breaks the ice for guests who don't know each other.

After the speeches, ask each table to nominate a speaker who will stand up and read their limerick to the guests. However, there is always a risk of offending someone. If in doubt, review each tables' work during the process to see how they are getting on. Be delicate, but generally you'll find people are self-censoring.

Not everyone opts to have cards and other messages read out. If a message is cordial yet predictable, it may dull the energy of the guests. Discuss it with the wedding couple beforehand. If messages are being read out, make sure you limit them.

MC: examples of what to say

Although the MC has a great deal of freedom to ad lib, the following examples are designed to give you an idea of what could be said. This will vary depending on the formality of the wedding.

Before the bridal party arrives at the top table

Once the guests are seated. 'Ladies and gentlemen, it's with great delight that I welcome you here this evening to celebrate the wedding of [BRIDE] and [GROOM].'

When the bridal party arrives at the top table

After asking the guests to be silent. 'Ladies and gentlemen! With your applause, please give a warm welcome to the parents of the bride and the parents of the groom! [SAME APPLIES TO THE REMAINDER OF THE

WEDDING PARTY – BEST MAN, MAID OF HONOUR, BRIDESMAIDS ETC.] Finally, please stand and welcome with your applause and cheers two very special, very happy, very newly married people – Mr and Mrs [SURNAME], the bride and groom!' [OR BRIDE AND BRIDE, GROOM AND GROOM].

After the meal is finished – the speeches

Tap a glass to get the guests' attention. 'Ladies and gentlemen, if I could have your attention for a moment … [WAIT FOR GENERAL SILENCE] thank you. I hope you enjoyed that fantastic meal and that all of you are content and full. I know I am – I've been trying to get out of my seat for 10 minutes. [PAT YOUR STOMACH AND MAKE A FACE TO SUGGEST YOU'VE OVEREATEN. PAUSE FOR LAUGHTER]

'If you have enjoyed the meal, then please join me in a round of applause for the staff here and in the kitchens. [PAUSE FOR APPLAUSE]

'How are your hands? Warm? [PAUSE AND SMILE] Good – because I'm warming you up for the main part of this evening, the speeches! You may have spotted a few very nervous faces up here. [POINT TO MAIN TABLES] If you have, then at least you know who will be giving a speech.

'If they think they're nervous, they should consider what it would have been like to be in [THE COUPLE'S] shoes earlier today. Although I have to say I was really surprised to see how relaxed they were. I guess when you're in love like they are today, what could possibly make you nervous? [PAUSE] Well, maybe an MC who rambles on and on ... [PAUSE FOR LAUGHTER OR HECKLES] Actually, speaking of rambling, I'd like to introduce to you a man who is famous for it. [PAUSE] Please put your hands together for the father of the bride!' [SIMILAR STRUCTURE FOR THE REMAINING SPEAKERS]

After the speeches

'Well I have to say those speeches made public speaking look easy. If any fool can do it, then the speakers tonight definitely proved it!' [PAUSE]

Introduce the cake cutting as the bride and groom move across to the cake. 'Ladies and gentlemen, the wedding couple have a hankering for cake right now and I believe they brought their own along and are going to tuck into it right now. You're more than welcome to take as many photos as you like!'

Introduce the first dance if applicable. 'I'd like to invite the wedding couple to take to the dance floor for the first dance of the evening. Please, give them your applause!' [CONTINUE ON TO INVITE THE REST OF THE WEDDING PARTY AND, FINALLY, THE GUESTS TO DANCE]

Time to go

Ask the guests to gather for the throwing of the bouquet. 'Ladies, and gentlemen too, please gather round as the bride is now ready to throw her bouquet. Good luck to all the unmarried ladies in the room!'

Ask the guests to assemble to bid farewell to the bride and groom. 'Thank you again for joining in the wedding celebrations and for putting up with me! I've never been heckled by such a polite crowd! But I want to thank you and hope that you've had a wonderful time.' [PAUSE]

'Well, it's time to bid farewell to Mr and Mrs [SURNAME] and wish them good luck. Please form a circle so the bride and groom can bid you all goodbye.'

Father of the bride

The first speech is traditionally made by the father of the bride. This stems from the historic notion that it is the bride's parents who pay for the wedding. Of course, that's not always the case today and the bridal couple often foot the bill themselves (sometimes with parents contributing). But if you are the father of the bride – or a designated representative – it's considered polite to let you speak first.

The father of the bride is asked to speak by the MC. You start your speech by thanking the guests for coming, and thanking those who have contributed to the wedding and those who have travelled a long distance to get there. Traditionally this is your opportunity to speak about your daughter and what she means to you – you're sharing how you feel about handing her over to the care of her partner. At the same time, be aware that you should also be speaking on behalf of her mother (if she is not delivering a speech herself).

Be open and honest. This is a wonderful chance for you to tell your daughter, and all assembled, how you feel about her. Talk about her life – the ups and downs. The core element of your speech should be a particular story from her past. It might encapsulate her entire character, reveal an aspect only a parent would remember with deep affection, or it might simply be a funny story – just make sure it doesn't require a lot of explaining.

If the anecdote is humorous, try to blend in some poignancy. Conversely, if your anecdote is emotionally stirring and beautiful, interweave it with some humour. Remember: the best speeches are a balance of both. Don't worry about coming across as too sentimental. This is a rare chance to do so, without being criticized!

The other main purpose of your speech is to welcome your new son-in-law officially into your family. Maybe recall when you first met him or occasions you and he (and maybe his family) have shared together. Giving some marriage advice in a humorous way also goes down well (see pages 74–75).

Speech contents

1   Thank the MC for his introduction. If the MC is the best man, it's nice to thank him for the wonderful job he has done.

2   Thank anyone who has contributed to the cost of the day.

3   The final thank you is to the guests for coming and especially to those who have travelled a long distance.

4   Tell a story or anecdote from your daughter's life – either one longer one or a couple of shorter ones (try to blend them together).

5   Traditionally the father of the bride says a few words on love and marriage. Some people prefer not to do this – understandably they don't want to appear to be preaching to the groom. However, there's nothing wrong with sharing some warm thoughts on marriage.

6   Say some words about the groom. What do you think of him and his family (especially his parents)? Is there something about him that has struck a chord with you? Tell him.

7   Don't forget to include your wife or partner, especially when wishing the new bride and groom a happy future together and when thanking people.

8   Finally, end by proposing a toast to the happy couple.

Advice

If there is no MC and some guests may not know you, you should introduce yourself.

If there is anyone who could not make it to the wedding (such as for serious health reasons) and they are close to the bride or groom, it's a polite touch to mention their absence and wish them well.

If there has been a recent death in the family, it's also considered fitting to remember that person on this day (especially if he or she were close to your daughter). Although for some it can be an emotionally difficult or sensitive issue to broach, it can also be touching if handled tactfully. (For more advice on this, see pages 54–55.)

Example

[TURN TO MC] 'Thank you [MC] for that flattering introduction and for the wonderful job you've done so far.

[TURN TO GUESTS] 'Ladies and gentlemen, the wonderful memory of today will remain with both myself [TURN TO WIFE] and [WIFE'S NAME] for the rest of our lives. It has been a perfect day. Knowing [BRIDE] and [GROOM] as I do, it's not surprising that it has turned out as well as it has. They have put a great deal of time and effort into preparing for it. I'd also like to take this opportunity to thank [NAMES OF THOSE WHO HELPED PLAN OR FUND THE WEDDING] for their deeply appreciated contribution to making this day what it is.

[TURN TO BRIDE] '[BRIDE] you look absolutely stunning today, darling. Your mother and I are incredibly proud of you.

[TURN TO GROOM] '[GROOM] you're a wonderful person and we're very honoured to welcome you into our family.

[BRIDE] thinks the world of you and I understand why. Seeing you both so happy together today just confirms what a perfect match you are.

[TURN TO GUESTS] 'Forgive this old man if you can, but it feels like not so long ago that [BRIDE]'s loud music was booming through the house. It used to drive me mad, that racket. Of course, being a teenager at the time she knew this and as a result turned the volume up even higher. Little did I realize back then that it would be because of her love for that same God-awful racket that she would meet [GROOM]. Maybe that music isn't so bad after all [PAUSE]. Actually, no – it is bad. However, I'll give it one good point – it was the first thing you both found in common.

'Yesterday, the list of things [BRIDE] and [GROOM] had in common was much greater and much deeper than when they first met. As of today, they have one more thing in common – they're married to each other.

'Of course, the things we have in common are great, but a man and a woman can also have their differences. And when it comes to marriage, I think these differences are often given too much prominence. Now this is where I can give some marital advice – I should know what I'm talking about, because [WIFE'S NAME] has been giving me marital advice for years! [PAUSE FOR LAUGHTER].

'As I was saying – I think the differences between a man and a woman or between any two people are given too much prominence. Living happily with our common ground is easy; living happily with our differences may seem difficult, but it can also be wonderful in its own way.

[TURN TO BRIDE AND GROOM] 'I think one of the many keys to a happy marriage is to cherish those differences, because they're just as much a part of the person you are in love with as those things you have in common. [PAUSE] This evening I see two extraordinary people who already have a wonderful respect for each other's differences. Why? [PAUSE] Because they're two people who have a great ability to let their hearts shine honestly.

'So, even though I don't think the newlyweds need me to wish them happiness for their future – I can see it there in them already – on behalf of [WIFE'S NAME] and myself, we both wish you a very long, healthy and incredibly happy future together.

[TURN TO GUESTS] 'And never the one to pass up a toast, and no toast is more worthwhile than this, please be upstanding and join me [RAISE YOUR GLASS] in a toast [TURN TO THE HAPPY COUPLE AND RAISE GLASS] to the bride and groom!'

Groom

The groom's speech traditionally comes after the father of the bride's. If the bride is not going to be giving her own speech, remember that your speech is given on her behalf as well. The groom's speech is also used to thank those who have contributed to the wedding either financially (such as parents, if the father of the bride hasn't already thanked them) or through their assistance (the best man, bridesmaids, ushers, flower girls and pageboys etc.).

Your speech is an opportunity to reflect on the event that has brought the guests together today. You can do this by relating how you and your wife first met. What went through your mind? Are there any interesting stories from the early days? Perhaps, from your first meal together? Or the day that you (or she!) popped the question?

Speech contents

1   If your wife is not going to be delivering her own speech, then it's a good idea to start your speech with, 'My wife and I …' This is a nice technique for drawing the guests in. After all, this is the very first opportunity amongst family and friends to use this phrase – a fitting place if ever there was one.

2   If you have been introduced to the guests by the MC, thank the MC for the introduction and for doing a great job.

3   Thank the father of the bride for his kind words and respond in kind to any compliments he has paid you in his speech. (See the 'Advice' section below for more on this.)

4   Thank the guests for coming – if the father of the bride hasn't already thanked those who have travelled some distance to get to the wedding, then you should.

5   Thank everyone for their generous wedding gifts.

6   It's always warm and polite to sincerely congratulate the bride's parents on doing a wonderful job of bringing her up.

7   Comment on how the day has gone so far (maybe use it as a link to the story of how you and your new wife first met).

8   Explain how you and your wife met. Who made the first move? Who proposed to whom?

9   Add in any humorous stories about your life together so far. If your new wife is not going to deliver a speech, make sure you devote a large part of your speech to her – tell her how you feel about her and what she means to you.

10 Turn your speech's direction towards the best man (especially if his speech is directly after yours). Thank him for accepting the role (and also if he is the MC) and maybe tell the guests you're dreading what he is going to say (which you probably will be).

11 Offer a toast to your beautiful wife – this gives the groom a very precious moment to step back with all those assembled and honour his new bride.

12 Finally, thank the bridesmaids on behalf of yourself and your new wife. Propose a toast to them from both of you.

Advice

If you have been introduced by the MC, listen out for any dig or joke he or she has flung at you in his or her introduction. Before you step up to speak, try to think of a nice comeback to respond with. A character assassination of the groom is traditional at most weddings, so be prepared to defend yourself!

If the father of the bride has said that he and his wife are proud to have you as a son-in-law then reply in kind. For example,

'Thank you for your kind words [FATHER-IN-LAW]. I'm very proud to be your son-in-law and promise not to let either you or [MOTHER-IN-LAW] down ...'

Congratulate the bride's parents on how well they've brought up their daughter, your wife. See it from their point of view – they've loved her, worked hard for her, fed her and supported her through every stage of her life so far. Hearing that the groom (their new son-in-law) appreciates this means a great deal to them, so let them know.

If the best man is not yet married, remind him that whatever he says about you today will come back to haunt him as you have a long and vengeful memory! It's a case of the last laugh and all that. This kind of humorous sparring can add a real humour to the speeches.

If someone couldn't attend the wedding because of illness, wish that person a speedy recovery.

If either of your, or the bride's, parents have passed away, consider tactfully mentioning that in the speech. (For advice on this subject, refer to the section called 'Discussing family or friends who have passed away', see pages 54–55.)

Some grooms' speeches also include a thank you to their own parents and/or any particularly close family or friends who've provided help.

Another idea that is sometimes used is for the bridal couple to make a speech together. Of course, this involves a lot of cooperation (what an opportunity to test your marital skills!). A joint speech would involve all the elements of the groom's speech contents (above) and a choice from the bride's speech contents. It can add a special touch to the speeches and give extra meaning to 'speaking for the both of you'. The amount of preparation and cooperation involved in a joint speech is probably why this technique is rarely used (you'll probably be busy enough just arranging the day itself). However, if you and your bride-to-be find the idea appealing, give it a go.

Example

[TURN TO FATHER OF THE BRIDE] 'Thank you [FATHER OF THE BRIDE] for your kind words and for welcoming me in to your family – it's an honour for me too. [PAUSE] I'd also like to thank you and congratulate you and [MOTHER OF THE BRIDE] on bringing up such a loving, caring, intelligent and beautiful daughter as [BRIDE]. I promise to deserve the praise that you have just given me.

[TURN TO GUESTS] 'Ladies and gentlemen, my wife and I [PAUSE] would like to thank you all for sharing this day with us and for your generous gifts. I also want to thank [MC] for his [OR HER] work and entertainment. [PAUSE] I'd also like to thank [BEST MAN] for keeping me calm and focused today, unlike on the stag night when he kept me legless and bleary-eyed. [PAUSE FOR LAUGHTER] Really though – you've been great. I say these nice things to you now because I know your speech will be full of nice things about me later! Won't it? [PAUSE FOR LAUGHTER]

[TURN TO BRIDESMAIDS] 'I'd also like to thank the ushers and the beautiful bridesmaids. Their help has made a real difference to our preparations.

[TURN TO YOUR PARENTS] 'Thank you too to my parents for all you've done for me. [PAUSE] It's terrible in a way, because now that I'm married I suppose I can't bring my washing home for mum to do, and because I believe in equality, I can't leave it for [BRIDE] to do. I might just have to learn how to do it myself. [FAKE SOB; PAUSE FOR LAUGHTER]

'I've left my most important thank you to last. My thank you is to that beautiful woman you may have seen standing next to me today who looks absolutely stunning.

[TURN TO BRIDE] 'Thank you for having me as your husband. Thank you for being the wonderfully funny, caring, enchanting and gorgeous woman that you are. [PAUSE] I love you.

[TURN TO GUESTS] 'The fact is I loved her from the start. But, being younger then, I was too daft to notice for about a week. I must have made a great impression on her because after we met, [BRIDE] went away for a week's holiday with her sister! [PAUSE] During that short span, I didn't realize what was wrong with me until [BEST MAN] began reminding me to eat and to stop staring into space and smiling stupidly.

'Maybe love is a happy illness wrapped up with its own cure. [PAUSE] It makes her happiness crucial to yours. Maybe that's what they mean about two becoming one. [PAUSE] That's why I look forward to our life together so much. [PAUSE]

'Well, before I slip back into that lovesick stupor again let me once again thank all of our wonderful wedding party. Please join with us in a well-deserved toast to the bridesmaids.' [RAISE GLASS]

Bride

It's not uncommon nowadays for the bride to stand up and give a speech. Unlike those of the more traditional speakers, the bride's speech has no huge expectation attached to it. As a result, the contents of your speech is completely up to you.

So, if it's not traditional for you to give a speech, why would you want to? Well, it is your special day too, so why not? It's an opportunity to respond to your husband's speech, to speak about what your husband means to you and to extend your personal and public thanks to those who've made the day possible. The suggested speech contents below are intended to give you some prompts to what you might say.

Speech contents

1 Thank those who've helped you prepare for the day – the groom should have already thanked the ushers and bridesmaids in his speech, but there's nothing wrong with you also thanking them again if you wish.

2 If your father has given the 'father of the bride' speech, then here's a nice opportunity for you to express to both your parents how you feel about them. Thank them for their support and for all they've done for you.

3 Describe your relationship with your parents and with any brothers or sisters you may have – humorous family stories always go down well with an audience.

4 Talk about the groom's parents – in traditional speeches, the groom's parents don't get a huge mention (except for in the 'father of the bride's' speech) so why not thank

them for bringing up their son so well and for welcoming you into their family?

5   You may have a funny anecdote about your husband, which provides some more room for humour. It could be from when you first met or early dates or even something that occurred during the wedding preparations.

6   Joking apart, this is also an opportunity for you to tell your husband what he means to you in front of your family and friends.

7   To finish, you could use an unusual but charming addition to the wedding toasts – thank the guests by toasting them on behalf of the wedding group.

Advice

If there is anybody special, such as a close friend, who has helped you during your life up to this point (for example during tough times) then this is a good opportunity to thank them.

Sometimes, the bride may wish to deliver a speech if her father is not present. This essentially means she's replacing the 'father of the bride's' speech. If this is the case, also refer to the 'father of the bride' chapter (see pages 19–23).

Example

'I'd like to thank my parents for all they've done for me and to thank [GROOM]'s family for welcoming me so warmly. I also want to thank the wedding party for making all the hard work seem so much easier.

[TO GUESTS] 'As you know, it's not traditional for the bride to make a speech. But I grew up with four older sisters, and as [GROOM] knows, I'm never shy about speaking my mind! [PAUSE FOR LAUGHTER] That's probably why I was stunned when [GROOM] proposed. There we were, sitting back on a quiet secluded beach watching the waves roll in. Then [GROOM] gets up, only he doesn't, he just rests on one knee. Before I could push him into the sand – which I would have done normally – he presents me with a ring and asks, "Will you marry me?" [PAUSE]

'I think the sun set before I finally answered him. [PAUSE] Not because I wasn't sure what to say and not because my mind was spinning. [PAUSE] I took my time because I wanted to enjoy that moment – to savour what it meant.

'And how did I answer him? There, with poor [GROOM] still on his bended knee starting to get pins and needles? [PAUSE] My "yes" came out in a flood of tears and I was a total mess … I was a mess and I was happy. But I'm glad I hung onto that special moment in our life – I wanted it to last forever.

'When I say that I'll love him my whole life it's not because it's easy to say such a thing – I say it because I know it's true. [PAUSE] That's what brought us here today [TURN TO GUESTS] and what brought you here too. So let me thank you all for coming and making our day extra special.'

Best man

Traditionally, it is the best man's speech that is the most anticipated one (sorry to scare you). Today the best man function can be fulfilled by a woman as well. If you're a natural showman, you'll probably lap up this role. If not, you'll still enjoy yourself more than your current apprehension is allowing you to believe is possible. Fear not – although the best man's speech is usually expected to get a laugh from the guests, people aren't anticipating a stand-up comedian.

If you're also acting as the MC, you'll already have warmed up a little, so remain relaxed and enjoy yourself. Remember, as best man, you are also speaking on behalf of the rest of the wedding assistants (the bridesmaids, ushers, pageboys, flower girls etc.).

Try to balance humour with tact, and don't be tempted to speak for too long.

Speech contents

1   If you are not also doubling up as the MC, thank the MC for their introduction then reply to the groom's toast to the bridesmaids on their behalf.

2   Thank the groom (and bride if she has also spoken) for their kind words about the wedding assistants. Also thank them for the honour of being chosen to be best man.

3   Traditionally the wedding couple give gifts to the wedding assistants. On behalf of them and yourself, thank the wedding couple for these gifts. Maybe joke that the gifts will not act as a bribe and stop you from making fun of the groom.

4   Tell a couple of funny stories and anecdotes about the groom. If you and the groom grew up together, touch on that – you could even run your stories as if you were recapping his life. Sometimes funny things happen during the wedding preparations and of course the stag night provides lots of ammunition too.

5   If you have any humorous anecdotes about the bride, include them too (unless a bridesmaid or maid of honour is going to be making a speech covering the bride's past).

6   If you have some funny stories, balance them with something poignant and touching. Don't be afraid to express your friendship.

7   Read out any cards or messages.

8   Thank the groom on behalf of the bridesmaids for his kind words, on behalf of yourself and the wedding assistants and give the bride and groom your best wishes for their future together.

9   Conclude your speech by announcing the cutting of the cake if there is no MC to do so, and ask the guests to raise their glasses in a toast to the bride and groom.

Advice

During your speech, make a point of addressing the wedding couple directly. Be kind to the bride and steer clear of the groom's previous relationships unless you're absolutely certain it will be received well. In any of your funny anecdotes about the groom, if there is a prop you can use, do so. Props enhance the hilarity of jokes or funny stories, especially those with a history such as props from childhood (a toy car, school bag or a letter they wrote as a child). (Refer to the 'Using humour' section; see pages 74–75.)

If you are already married and your best man was the current groom, use this as an opportunity for sweet revenge!

Example

'Ladies and gentlemen, before I start, I'd like to take this opportunity on behalf of the bridesmaids, to thank [BRIDE] and [GROOM] for their kind words and their considerate gifts. Although the CD you gave me looks exactly like the one I loaned [GROOM] last year. [PAUSE FOR LAUGHTER]

[TURN TO THE GROOM] 'Personally though, I want to thank you for asking me to be your best man. I think you're insane, but thank you – it's a real honour.

[TURN TO GUESTS] 'I'm sure you've all been waiting for my speech because as you know, the best man has a great job. I get to make [GROOM] squirm for a few minutes. Now, if he starts squirming, don't feel sorry for him – he squirms like that a lot. It's a physical defect, but [BRIDE] tells me it doesn't bother her at all for some reason! [PAUSE FOR LAUGHTER]

'To be honest, despite what you might be expecting, I won't be telling you about the time [GROOM] walked around for a whole day at school with his flies open. No big deal you may think – not if you're wearing underwear, which he wasn't. [PAUSE FOR LAUGHTER] That means I won't tell you how the whole school knew about it by the end of the day. And if I don't tell you that, then I won't tell you that's how he got stuck with the nickname of "Draughty" for years. [PAUSE]

'So I won't be telling tales like that. Instead I'll explain the kind of chap [GROOM] is by way of demonstration.

[PAUSE] [GROOM] is sensitive, caring and nurturing. [PRODUCE OLD TEDDY BEAR FROM UNDER THE TABLE] See? Look at the condition this teddy is in. Scary, isn't it? And do you know where I found this? In his bedroom! [PAUSE FOR LAUGHTER] So it's not surprising he found a match in [BRIDE]. She is just as caring and nurturing as he is.

'I think they both look fantastic today. In fact I think they will look fantastic even when they're old and wrinkly. They'll look fantastic because they'll still be in love. [PAUSE]

'With that said, on behalf of myself and all the wedding party, may I wish [BRIDE] and [GROOM] a life together even better than [GROOM]'s teddy's, a life that is long, filled with laughter, good health and fortune.

'Please join me in proposing a toast to the bride and groom!'

Mother of the bride

Although it's not traditional for the mother of the bride to deliver a speech, there is nothing wrong with you doing so. Your speech is very flexible, so if there's something special you want to say about your daughter and the person whom she has just married, this is a perfect opportunity to do so.

Speech contents

1   Thank the MC for the introduction.
2   Talk about your daughter and your relationship with her.
3   Relate any significant or humorous memories of her as a child – you could use visual props, for example.
4   Talk about the groom and what you think of him and his family.
5   Maybe provide some motherly advice with a balance of sincerity and humour. It should come across as loving advice.
6   As the groom's new mother-in-law, why not use that unfairly infamous title to crack a joke? Threaten him with the prospect of spending lots of quality time together. You could even promise to visit every second day, and then tell him that his mother will be visiting every other day. This 'motherly conspiracy' can be a very funny addition to the speeches.
7   Whatever you frighten him with, end it on a sincere and friendly note, welcoming him into your family.
8   Finish by wishing both of them a happy and healthy future together.

Advice

If you are also filling in for the father of the bride, please refer to the speech contents on pages 19–23.

If there is no MC, then introduce yourself. You could do this casually by saying something such as, 'As [BRIDE]'s mother ...' To add some humour, maybe you could say, 'As [BRIDE]'s long-suffering mother ...'

Example

'It's not often a mother gets the undivided attention of her children without having to threaten to send them to their room. Of course, it's been a very long time since I've had to do that. Just like it's been a long time since I read her fairytales at bedtime but it feels like yesterday – in fact, I think it was yesterday! [PAUSE FOR LAUGHTER]

'I have to say, [BRIDE] was generally a well-behaved child. I say "generally" because when she did get out of hand, oh boy, did she put up a fight! From the start [BRIDE] was the kind of person who stood her ground.

'I remember a few staring matches we had, especially over brussel sprouts – she absolutely hated them! On one occasion I told her she couldn't leave the table until she had eaten them. She refused and cheekily told me she'd stay until ... [TURN TO BRIDE] what were the words, darling? [PAUSE] Until they "rotted on the plate". [PAUSE FOR LAUGHTER] [TURN TO GUESTS] She went on to describe what they would look like and smell like when they finally rotted. It was disgusting! [PAUSE] When she finished her description we just sat there staring each other down ... for nearly half an hour. [PAUSE] So who won? Hard to say, really. In the end she ate one of the two sprouts while putting on a face as if she were eating worms. It was threat, then negotiation and a diplomatic solution. [PAUSE]

'When I think back on that now, I look upon her with pride. I knew then that [BRIDE] was never going to be someone to be bossed around. At the same time she has always had a deeply caring heart, especially for people feeling down, so it's no surprise she ended up being a psychiatrist!

[TURN TO GUESTS] 'Ah, children. Predictable and unpredictable. They can drive you up the wall but they can make you tearful when you think of how much they mean to you. Then suddenly, they find a certain someone to love and who loves them, in this case, [GROOM].

'When [PARTNER] and I first met [GROOM], we could see that they had each other figured out already. They looked as if they'd been together for decades. [GROOM] is a kind, warm and considerate man. It's not surprising really, especially since we've got to know his parents, [MOTHER AND FATHER OF THE GROOM]. [PAUSE]

'As I said, your daughter finds someone to love and who loves her in return and, before you know it, they're making their own home. It doesn't make me sad, though. [BRIDE] has grown into a woman who I'm incredibly proud to know.

[TURN TO BRIDE] 'And if I don't get to tell her to go to her room or read her fairytales these days, maybe I can at least say this: [BRIDE] I hope you and your groom live happily ever after.'

Maid or matron of honour

It is not traditional for the maid or matron of honour to give a speech but you can if you and the bride both wish it. Unlike the best man's speech, yours is not constrained by traditional content such as having to thank everybody. Instead, while the best man gets to have a bit of fun at the groom's expense, you can poke fun at the bride. You probably have some great stories to tell.

Speech contents

1 Thank the MC for the introduction.
2 Thank the bride and groom for inviting you to speak.
3 Give a humorous description of your relationship with the bride.
4 Describe her as a person (balance it with humour and sincerity).
5 If you have any funny stories about the bride or about the bride and groom together, tell them.
6 Offer the bride some advice on marriage (especially if you are the matron of honour) – again this can be comedic.
7 Finish by telling her what she means to you and wish the couple a happy future together.

Advice

Blend the contents into each other. For example, your description of the bride as a person could lead into a funny story you have about her past. Although the golden rule concerning jokes about the bride is that they should be made with extreme caution, you have the added advantage of having a special relationship with her, so you have a bit more leeway.

Example

'I'd like to thank [BRIDE] for asking me to be the maid/matron of honour and inviting me to speak. I've known [BRIDE] since we first started school together and it was a friendship set to last from that first day.

'As you know, the first day of school affects people in different ways. Some are silent with shock. Some are too busy picking their noses and gazing around to realize what they've just been thrown into. Others find it all too much and sit there bawling their eyes out calling for their mummies.

'[BRIDE] and I were part of that last group. Our mothers had probably explained what this "school" place was but, you know, they might as well have been telling us we were going to Mars – well it certainly felt like that to us.

'There we were, two little strangers sitting next to each other, crying our heads off in a new and scary world. [PAUSE] Then [BRIDE] looked at me and I looked at her. She stopped crying, put her hand on my shoulder and said, "It's okay. We'll be fine. We're at school." [PAUSE]

'That says an awful lot about [BRIDE]. You could be lost at night in a beaten up old hire car in the mountains of Laos and she'd smile reassuringly and say, "It's okay. We'll be fine. We're in Laos." Which really happened when we went backpacking around South-east Asia six years ago!

[PAUSE FOR LAUGHTER] Of course, hearing where we were didn't really help, but hearing her say it as if it was all perfectly normal did. She's one in a million. [PAUSE]

'That's why when [BRIDE] told me she and [GROOM] were going to get married I thought, "That makes a lot of sense!" [GROOM] is also "one in a million". Now they're two in a million and I'm honoured to count them both as friends.

[TURN TO GROOM] '[GROOM], I'm sure you'll look after my [BRIDE] and I know she'll look after you.

'I hope you'll have a wonderful life together, and if the road gets difficult or bumpy along the way, as marriages can, just say to each other, "It's okay. We'll be fine. We're married!"'

Mother of the groom/ Father of the groom

When there is an opportunity for either the mother or father of the groom to say a few words, it provides a nice opening not only to express what the wedding means to them but also to welcome the bride into their family. The speech structure is basically the same whether you are the mother or father.

You could rely on aspects of your role as mother or father to flavour your speech, as each of you will have your own gender's take on life, marriage and other relevant matters.

Speech contents

1 Thank the MC for the introduction.
2 If the father of the bride has already thanked those who contributed to the cost or organization of the wedding, there is really no need to thank them again – instead offer some warm words to the father and mother of the bride.
3 Talk about your son – tell the guests any memorable stories that define his character (they could be humorous or poignant). Most of all tell your son how you feel about him.
4 Sincerely welcome the bride into your family.
5 Talk about your new daughter-in-law. What impression has she made on you? What effect has she had on your son?
6 Finish by wishing the happy couple a wonderful life together.

Advice

If there is no Master of Ceremonies, begin by introducing yourself to the guests.

A humorous technique called the 'motherly conspiracy' was mentioned in the mother of the bride speech (see page 36). This conspiracy is a great way of linking a joke between both mothers but it could also be arranged to fit any jokes that the fathers come up with.

Example

'Ladies and gentlemen, for those of you who don't know me, I'm [GROOM]'s dad. You may have recognized me by the bags under my eyes. [PAUSE] Some people don't like having wrinkles, but I don't mind them. In fact I'm proud of these bags under my eyes. I like to think of them as medals earned in the line of duty. [PAUSE]

'That duty started on [DATE OF GROOM'S BIRTH] – the day [GROOM] was born. My comrade-in-arms was my wife [WIFE'S NAME] who eventually became General! [TURN TO WIFE] Well, my love, you deserved it, after all you carried him and went through the labour, something I certainly couldn't have done!

[TURN TO GUESTS] 'When [GROOM] was born, I had no real idea how long my parenting tour of duty would last. After six months of nappy changing and washing I knew the campaign would go on for a long, long time. As [GROOM] grew older, the whole idea of an end to this tour seemed to vanish and eventually I got to the stage where I never wanted it to end. [PAUSE]

'I got to see our son grow from a nursery school terror who looked up women's dresses to a young child who seemed completely fascinated by the world around him. Of course my admiration had its limits, especially when he tried making his own rocket fuel when he was eight. [PAUSE FOR LAUGHTER AND TURN TO GROOM] Oh, you remember, do you? Good!

[TURN TO GUESTS] 'You see, we used to have this old barbecue and [GROOM] thought it would make the perfect launching pad for his rocket with his new "rocket fuel".

'While [WIFE'S NAME] and I were working in the front garden, [GROOM] had fuelled and primed his rocket on his barbecue launching pad ... right next to one of the back windows of the house. [PAUSE] We didn't know that his experimental fuel was made out of everything with a "highly-flammable" label. [PAUSE]

'The first thing we heard was the biggest bang you've ever heard in your life, followed by glass breaking and the sound of the barbecue going through the back door! [PAUSE FOR LAUGHTER] Well, as you can see, he lived, although we could have strangled him. Still, even then I didn't want this tour of duty that is parenting to end. [PAUSE]

[TURN TO BRIDE] 'Then one day years later [GROOM] came home with this brilliant girl. Since then we've got to know [BRIDE] well and I don't think [WIFE'S NAME] or I could say enough good things about her. We couldn't ask for a more honest and charming daughter-in-law.

[TURN TO FATHER AND MOTHER OF THE BRIDE] 'The same can be said for her wonderful parents with whom, it's a pleasure to say, we have become great friends.

[TURN TO GROOM] 'Son, you've found yourself a terrific wife, friend and partner in life and your mum and I are incredibly happy for you both. We wish both of you the very, very best for your future. [PAUSE]

[TURN TO GUESTS] 'As for my tour of duty ... well, no parent ever stops being a parent, do they? Not really. [PAUSE] So when I look in the mirror in the morning, at these medals, [POINT TO BAGS UNDER EYES] I just think about [GROOM]. I think about all the years we've spent together. I think of the man he's become, whom I admire so much [PAUSE] and I also think about that bloody rocket fuel sometimes too! [PAUSE FOR LAUGHTER]

'No matter what, he still makes me smile. So, on behalf of [WIFE] and I, good luck to you both for your new life together.'

Close friend or relative

Sometimes a close friend or relative of either the bride or groom is invited to make a speech. This may be because they have a particularly special relationship with that person. (Note: if you are filling in for the father of the bride, base your speech on that role instead of this one.)

As a person dear to one (or both) of the wedding couple, you are essentially free to say what you feel about them, who they are and what this day means to you as a result.

Speech contents

1   Thank the MC for introducing you.
2   Briefly explain who you are and your relationship with the wedding couple.
3   Thank the bride and groom for inviting you to speak.
4   Discuss what the bride or groom and, as a result, what the day means to you.
5   If you have any particularly strong memories of the bride or groom, or funny anecdotes, tell them.
6   Talk about their new spouse and how they seem together.
7   Maybe give them some light-hearted marital advice.
8   Finally, give them your best wishes for their future together.

Advice

Whatever you choose to say, remember that your words are intended to provide another view of the person you're speaking of.

Example

'Thank you [BRIDE] and [GROOM] for asking me to speak on your wedding day.

[TURN TO GUESTS] 'As [BRIDE]'s aunt, seeing her with [GROOM] today was one of the loveliest sights of my entire life. I really mean it. [PAUSE] I've known [BRIDE] since she was born and the partner she has found in [GROOM] makes absolute sense.

'[BRIDE] thrives on untidiness. [GROOM] likes things to be orderly. [BRIDE] hates cooking but cooks like a chef. [GROOM] loves cooking but, as he once told me, he cooks like a mechanic. So, what is it that brings these opposites together? Is love that strong? [TURN TO BRIDE AND GROOM] It obviously is. [PAUSE]

[TURN TO GUESTS] 'But I also think every marriage has a certain thing that makes two particular people click. In the case of [BRIDE] and [GROOM], they aren't only husband and wife or lovers or partners – they're also best friends. [PAUSE]

'They are two people who might disagree on this or that, but never let anything get between the bond they've created. [PAUSE] That's why today was one of the loveliest sights of my life – I saw harmony. And if [BRIDE] and [GROOM] can walk through life and marriage with that harmony, then, as I think you can already see, they are set for a beautiful life together. [TURN TO BRIDE AND GROOM] I wish you both a long and happy marriage!'

Alternative speakers

An alternative or proxy speaker is needed when the original person is unable to attend the wedding – for whatever reason – and deliver their speech. There are various reasons why a speech role would need to be filled by a proxy. The original, intended person may:

- Have been unable to attend due to illness.
- Not be attending the wedding due to personal reasons.
- Have passed away.

Filling in for a person unable to attend due to illness

If this occurs, it usually happens very close to or on the wedding day. If you are the one filling in, you're probably panicking about the speech – well, don't. There are two ways you can get through this.

Firstly, if the original person has to leave (or whatever the case may be), try to contact them. They may already have completed their speech, which could make your life a bit easier. In that case, you could simply give a short introduction briefly explaining why the original speaker was unable to attend, then read their speech. This depends on the sensitivity of the person's absence and if you do mention it, be diplomatic and smooth it over with some humour. If you wanted to, you could even modify their speech so that it comes from you. After all, you may have been requested to jump in by the wedding couple because you were the perfect choice.

Alternatively, you may wish to write your own speech from scratch. This all depends on how much time is left before the wedding. If there are a couple of days left, you should be able to come up with something. (Make sure you also refer to 'Planning and writing the speech', pages 51–77.) Depending on the role you've been asked to fill, base your speech on that particular role's chapter.

Finally, don't forget to include an apology from the original speaker. If their absence is due to illness, add in your wishes for a speedy recovery.

Filling in for someone who won't be attending due to personal reasons

When this occurs, it normally involves family members who may not be attending for historic family reasons. If you are filling in for this person, base your speech on the chapter covering the role they would be expected to perform.

As this is a sensitive subject (especially on a wedding day), it's obviously better not to discuss the reasons for the person's absence in your speech – only add that you were honoured to be asked to perform this role. As for the role itself, alter any specific elements to reflect your relationship with the bride and groom.

Filling in for a person who has passed away

How you approach your speech depends on how long ago that person passed away (the speech will be especially sensitive if it occurred very recently). However, it is not as difficult a task as it might seem – base your speech on that particular role's chapter. Alter the contents and tone of the speech to reflect what you want to say (based on your relationship with the bride and/or groom).

For more information on discussing someone who has passed away, see the relevant section ('Discussing family or friends who have passed away') on pages 54–55.

Planning and writing the speech

Here you'll learn how to plan and prepare what
you want to say in your speech.

Begin by creating an outline to set the structure
before writing it properly.

Once written, you can then summarize
it and transfer it to cue cards.

Planning and preparation

You've already begun your planning and preparation by reviewing the details of the role of your speech. The rest of the process will involve deciding what you want to say by choosing the memories and personal words you want to include, and creating a speech outline.

Speech writing considerations

Before you start, there are a number of aspects to speech-giving to bear in mind.

Order of speeches

Speeches were originally a short simple toast of 'to the bride and groom'. This toast eventually grew into 'a few words' and finally a full speech where the speakers offered their best wishes to the newly married couple. The traditional order of speeches has remained and is as follows:

- Father of the bride: opening speech, closing with the proposal of a toast to the bride and groom.
- Groom: response to the toast, speech and proposal of a second toast to the bridesmaids (on behalf of both himself and his new wife).
- Best man: response to the toast (on behalf of the bridesmaids), speech and reading out cards and messages. Announcing the cutting of the cake if applicable, and proposal of a toast to the bride and groom.

The wedding couple should arrange the order of the speeches well in advance. The main reason, from a speechwriter's perspective, is to find out who comes before you and who will be introducing whom. Of course you can always make an adjustment, but that's not exactly what you want to be doing at the last minute, is it?

Nowadays, the sequence (and number) of speeches varies. This is something for the wedding couple to decide on as part of their planning. You can never go wrong by sticking with the traditional model. If more people will be speaking, it's usually better to include them after the best man.

Here are a few final pieces of advice about planning the order of speeches:

- Always hold speeches after the meal has finished, when energy levels are at their highest – speeches given to an audience on an empty stomach are not appreciated. The guests (and the wedding party) have been on the go for hours but once they've eaten, they're ready to relax and listen.
- Don't get carried away and have too many people making speeches – it will bore the guests.
- The more speeches you have, the shorter each speech should be to balance the overall duration (this does not include the three traditional speakers).
- If at all possible, avoid sudden last-minute requests by people wanting to make a speech – the thing you're trying to avoid is the ad lib speaker. An exception to this could be if the married couple are happy to let them speak and that person has prepared something.
- It's a good idea to have an MC manage the order of the speeches and introduce the next speaker.

Deciding on the length of the speech

Although there is no golden rule for a speech's duration, less is often more. Three to four minutes is considered the norm and some people even prefer very short speeches, which are essentially stretched out toasts that last about one minute.

Don't allow your speech to ramble, and shy away from complicated anecdotes. Still, speech length really depends on how the reception is planned and you should discuss this with the other speakers and the wedding couple.

Ethnic and cultural considerations

Many marriages are between couples from diverse cultural and ethnic backgrounds. This is an important consideration when writing a speech. The same goes for deciding on the order of the speeches.

If the married couple come from different ethnic backgrounds, ask if their culture has any particular marriage customs for speeches. For example, some European cultures traditionally have the father of the groom speak before the father of the bride.

The rule is to ask. Not only is this extra cultural consideration polite, it could also have a profoundly positive effect on the family and guests assembled.

Discussing family or friends who have passed away

Wedding speeches are a way of celebrating the day itself. That's why many people find it difficult or awkward to mention in their speech a close friend or family member who has passed away. This is completely understandable and the choice is entirely yours.

If on this very special day you wish to remember someone you have lost, there is nothing wrong with doing so. The general rule is simply to be tactful and respectful. It's a delicate matter, but handled gently it allows you to include the memory of this person in the day. It can be a very touching, kind and respectful inclusion – especially if that person would have been a close and important guest if they were with you all on the day.

Of course, much depends on the circumstances and the sensitivities of others present (and your personal beliefs). That's why it is a good idea to discuss this subject with those closest to the person concerned first. If you decide to go ahead, bear these considerations in mind:

- Speak about the person as you would have spoken about them when they were alive.
- Depending on how well you knew the person (and if you're comfortable with it) comment on what they might have said on the day.
- Don't be afraid to be humorous when recalling them – especially if the person was a really funny character.
- Don't dwell on their loss, cherish the fact you knew them.
- Be wary of your words upsetting anyone or diminishing the general mood of a day intended for celebration.
- Be aware of causing any cultural or religious offence – in some cultures, discussing such matters at a wedding is considered disrespectful, painful or incredibly poor etiquette.

Once you've finished speaking about them, it's important to bring the guests back to the moment and the celebration. This is not discourteous; it ensures that the celebratory mood is not affected.

If this is a second marriage

If the bride and groom have been married before, you may feel uncomfortable saying anything about that marriage. The general rule is to avoid mentioning any previous relationships and the same goes for a previous marriage. It may cause offence and even detract from the uniqueness of the day for the wedding couple. The wedding is their day and the past is in the past.

If there are children present

If the bride or groom has a child/children present from a previous relationship or marriage it's obviously important not to hurt their feelings. The best advice is still not to mention the ex-partner (the child's biological father or mother). However, do make sure the children are mentioned. This is especially important in the groom's (and/or bride's) wedding speech. In that case, it's vital to make the child feel welcome and included.

Consider the age of the child and how he or she may perceive your words. If both the bride and groom have children from a previous marriage, ensure any mention of them is balanced. Children are keenly aware of favouritism. Remember: the wedding means the beginning of a new life for children in such circumstances, too.

Liaise with the wedding party

Before writing your speech, it's a good idea to find out in what order the speeches will be given. The wedding couple may also have a set idea about how long they want the speeches to be. Some weddings have more speakers than others, which will affect your speech's duration and content.

Always keep your audience in mind

Although you're addressing your speech to specific people on the wedding day, you need to keep all of the wedding guests in mind. It may seem an obvious point but it's actually one of the biggest flaws in wedding speeches.

For example, if you recall a funny event which is a private joke among only a couple of the guests, the rest of the audience may feel left out. Not only will you (and your private joke group) be laughing alone, you may also alienate the audience.

Use the opportunity to be as open as you wish

Your speech is a rare chance, when you have the undivided attention of your friends and relatives, to tell your loved ones how you feel about them: how much you love them and what they mean to you.

I recall one father of the bride who had always felt awkward and shy about publicly expressing his feelings for his daughter. In his speech he wore his heart on his sleeve in a way he'd never done before. There certainly were a lot of wet eyes and touched smiles. For him and his daughter, it was one of the most special moments they had shared. So make the most of it. Of course, don't get too emotional – after all, you don't want to turn the wedding into a wailing session or turn yourself into a blubbering mess.

What do you want your speech to say

Other than the details you've already identified in 'Speech contents' (pages 9–49), you will need brief lists of stories or anecdotes about the bride or groom and what they mean to you. You'll be using these stories to create the core of your speech – the parts that bring a loving or laughing tear to the eyes of the guests.

So let's get started. You'll need a notepad or note cards, pencil and rubber. You'll also need peace and quiet. Yes, that means turn off the TV and lock yourself away somewhere relaxing and quiet where you won't be disturbed every few minutes.

There are three main elements to wedding speeches. How much of each element you use is up to you because you're the one who is going to be writing and delivering the speech. The three elements of a speech we'll go through are:

a Standard and traditional content that should be covered by your role on the day.

b Poignant, humorous or significant anecdotes, stories and memories.

c How you feel about the people you are writing about.

Remember: you only have a couple of minutes to speak on the day. When you're preparing the speech outline, you'll only be selecting a handful of items from the lists to include in the speech, so don't get too carried away writing pages and pages. Your speech shouldn't be long enough to be available in leading bookshops! Try to keep your lists relatively short.

a Standard and traditional content

On the top of your new page write the heading 'TRADITIONAL THINGS IN MY SPEECH' in block capitals.

You have already found out in 'Speech contents' (pages 9–49) how your role's speech is traditionally structured, along with its contents. Remember that these days, wedding speeches are far more flexible and personal, so it's really all up to you. Copy down the speech contents you want to use or have been asked to use in your speech. Once you're finished, put that card or page to one side.

b Anecdotes, stories and memories

On the top of your new blank page, write the heading 'STORIES' in block capitals. Relax. Clear your mind.

Picture the people your speech will be about. Picture them as you normally see them. Think back as long as they've been in your life and replay memories you have of them. Some memories will obviously stand out above others.

On your notepad, write down the memories coming to you. It can be in single words, phrases or a couple of sentences recalling special, humorous or important events in the bride or groom's life. Don't worry about exact words or profound statements, just write them as they come. Leave a line between each idea on the page.

Write on only one side of the page and try to keep your list to one page. Remember to rub out mistakes, rather than scratching them out. Neater notes make for easy referencing when you're creating your outline later on.

To help trigger some memories, have a look through the following words and phrases:

• Birth	• Birthdays
• School	• Meeting for the first time
• Sports	• First impressions
• Painting	• First car

- Dates
- Animals
- Work

- Parties
- Holiday and travel
- Garden

A great way of getting the full picture of an event is to have a word with friends or family members. They'll either add an extra angle to the story or maybe even prompt another one. Don't get too carried away – relating memories in a speech can occupy a large amount of your speaking time. It's recommended that you distil your list down to one or two of the 'best' memories.

How do you know which are the best stories for your speech? Avoid ones requiring a lot of explanation. It's your choice, but there are two types of memories that work well in wedding speeches:

- Events illustrating to the guests the character, qualities and life of those you're speaking about.
- Events illustrating your feelings for them.

You may even find that certain memories sum up both of the above. Use the ones that work best for you. Once you're finished, put that page or card to one side.

c How you feel about them

On the top of your new page write the heading 'HOW I FEEL ABOUT THEM' in block capitals.

Picture yourself at the coming wedding. Picture the people you're going to be speaking about. Blot out any images of chatting guests, sounds or laughter. You're happily alone with the people you'll be speaking about and to – no-one else.

What do they mean to you?

What do you want to say to them on this important day in their lives?

On your notepad or card, write down what pops into your head about how you feel. Again, it may be in single words, phrases or a couple of sentences and may express how you feel about them especially on their big day. Don't worry about exact words or profound statements. Leave a blank line between each thought.

Now that this list is complete, re-read it and put it to one side with the others.

Creating the outline of the speech

Now that you have at least three pages or cards of lists, creating the outline structure is straightforward enough:

- Lay down the traditional structure (as you've modified it to your requirements).
- Figure out where each of the memories you've chosen will go in the outline.
- Blend in some words expressing how you feel about the people you are writing about.

Lay down the base structure

The best way to start is by using the traditional elements for your role. Feel free to try various versions of the outline until you're happy it covers everything you want to say.

- On a new blank page, write the heading 'OUTLINE'.
- Draw a line down the left side of the page and mark a bullet point at the top of the line and write out the first item from your 'Traditional things in my speech' list (you should have already established the order you want to use).
- Leave a gap of two blank lines below the first one, mark another bullet and write out the second item from the list and so on.
- Once that's done, you'll be looking at the basic outline of your speech.
  Now it's time to add the spice!

Add your anecdotes

- Look at the speech outline – you should have one or two places for stories and memories.
- Refer to your 'Stories' list and copy the anecdotes or memories that you have chosen into the speech outline.
- Look at the outline and consider where you'd like to include your points, touching on how you feel about them – you'll probably find this section works better when blended into your anecdotes or throughout your written speech script.

Review the speech outline

Now it's time to relax and clear your mind again. Take your time and read through the outline. Think about how it feels. Are you happy with the flow of it? Don't worry too much about how it sounds yet – leave that for the writing stage. Move things around if you want to.

Remember: you don't have to stick to the traditional structure if you don't want to. The only elements that shouldn't really change are the toasts and the thank yous.

Writing the speech

Now that you have completed the speech outline, you have a good structure to start writing from. Before you start, I have some encouraging news for you: this part is far easier than you may think.

By the end of this chapter, you will have a completed speech script. We'll get there by using the speech outline as the scaffolding on which to build around. This chapter will explain:

- 10 golden rules of speech writing.
- The process of writing the speech.
- Hooking the audience from the first line.
- Language and how to draw in the audience with rhythm, pace and flow.
- Using humour.
- Using quotations (from poetry, proverbs and famous people.)
- Deciding on the length of the speech.
- Using symbolism and creating pictures.
- Being expressive and poignant.
- Closing the speech.

The golden rules of writing a wedding speech

Behind every speech there are golden rules that have helped many a speechwriter hold it together well. These golden rules can be referred to at any time while you're writing. Some are common sense, the rest are dealt with in detail in this section.

1 Write in your natural voice. You are speaking to those who know you and hearing a familiar voice at a wedding,

speaking openly and honestly about their loved ones, is naturally eloquent and touching.

2   Write from the heart and give your words due meaning.

3   Shy away from romanticising the couple or their past, be honest while being discreet.

4   Don't be afraid to say emotional and poignant things – it's a wedding and you're allowed to.

5   Throw in some humour.

6   Write as much as you need to (time permitting) and make every word count.

7   Avoid repetition.

8   The best speeches inform and involve an audience.

9   Remember to follow your speech outline.

10   Don't offend your audience (especially the wedding couple!).

Writing the speech: from outline to script to cue card

To create the final speech you will write the script from the speech outline and then reduce the script to a cue card.

A script is actually the proper name for a speech written out word for word. A cue card is that same script, reduced to point form. The reason you shouldn't simply read from the entire script on the day is straightforward.

Picture this: a speaker steps up to the microphone and for four minutes reads from a prepared speech without raising their eyes from the page. By the end, half of the room looks as if they've been drugged and the other half looks as if they wish they were.

You've probably experienced this. The speech sounds monotonous because the speaker is purely concentrating on reading the words – they fail to engage the audience's interest. Reading straight from a script can strip words of meaning and sound unnatural. The last thing you want is to sound as if you are reading from a prepared speech (yes, that is the irony). That's why rehearsing the speech using cue cards (to be used on the day) will deliver a much better result.

Before you start the first line, you'll need to familiarize yourself with the rules of writing a speech. By the end of this chapter, you'll be wondering what you were worrying about.

Starting the speech: how to grab the audience from the first line

Ah, the first line. Your first line is what professional writers of all varieties call 'the hook'. Your first line has to capture the audience's attention and get them immediately interested. It's then a case of holding their interest and closing the speech tidily.

Now, back to the first line and the hook. This is your opening comment and statement and there are various types of hooks you can use:

- A famous and/or literary quotation.
- Humour.
- Anniversary links to the day.
- Bracketing the first and last lines of the speech.

A famous/literary quotation

Quotations can come from writers, philosophers, lovers or all three. In a wedding speech, the quotations you use should relate to love, marriage, friendship or family. Has anyone ever said something profound or touching to you about these subjects? Maybe you know of a line from a book, film or poem?

The wonderful thing about humanity is that we've written vast amounts on love. This isn't surprising, as love is the steady star we sail our lives by (you can quote me on that!). You'll find many sources for quotations – in the reference and poetry sections of a bookshop or on the internet (see page 93) .

When you've found a quotation, blend it into the first point of your speech. Don't waste time explaining the background of the quotation (the writer or the book etc.). The opening line must be clear and catchy. This is the first line, so you can't afford to throw in extra information that will detract from the meaning and message of the quotation.

Example

'Ladies and gentlemen, a man once wrote, "Love creates a past which envelops us, as if by enchantment." Today we come together to celebrate and witness that very same enchantment gently envelop [BRIDE] and [GROOM] in marriage. [PAUSE] I believe love hasn't only created their past – it has created a beautiful future together for them …

'Ladies and gentlemen, it is said, "Absence sharpens love, [PAUSE] presence strengthens it." [PAUSE] Seeing [BRIDE] and [GROOM] earlier today and here now provides the best example of love's strength one could ever hope to see …

'Ladies and gentlemen, E. M. Forster once wrote, "Love is a great force in private life; it is indeed the greatest of all things." I couldn't agree more with him after having the honour of witnessing the marriage today of [BRIDE] and [GROOM].

'Ladies and gentlemen, we are born seeking love. [PAUSE] Well, Oscar Wilde advised us, "When you really want love, you will find it waiting for you." And I believe [BRIDE] and [GROOM] did find it waiting for them – there in each other, [PAUSE] at the ceremony today and here, right at this moment.'

You could even open with a poem. This is especially poignant in a groom's speech (or a bride's). The best advice if using a poem is to choose a very short one or use the most striking verse. It allows you to start the speech in a less traditional way.

Example

'"She is the promise/given by the stroke/of a calming breeze/in hills bath'd by love's first sunrise." Ladies and gentlemen, a sunrise brings hope, beauty and promise. Tomorrow will be our first sunrise together as husband and wife. [PAUSE] The sun first rose for me the moment [BRIDE] and I met.'

Poetry is used more and more these days, but use it only if you feel comfortable with it and it describes how you feel.

Bracketing the speech

This is where the first lines connect with the last lines of your speech, bringing it full circle.

Example

'Ladies and gentlemen, when [BRIDE] was five years old she asked me what makes the sun shine. She asked dozens of those questions day after day. [YOUR WIFE] and I gave the best answers we could, but she sometimes looked back at us as if we were a little slow. [PAUSE FOR LAUGHTER] But, as she grew up, [BRIDE] became the one with the answers, and we asked the questions.

'Finally, just a year ago, [GROOM] asked her a real cracker of a question. [PAUSE] And wouldn't you know it – she had the answer! [PAUSE FOR LAUGHTER] Well, I'm proud and happy to say that is why we're here today ...

'After all the planning they put into today, I'm not surprised it has gone as wonderfully smoothly as it has. It seemed as if everything happened on cue – the ceremony, the seating – even the sun seemed to shine to schedule. [PAUSE] Which reminds me, [BRIDE] all those years ago, I don't think I answered your question about what makes the sun shine. [PAUSE] Well, seeing you and [GROOM] together today, I think the answer speaks for itself.'

Then the toast would be proposed. Bracketing can be difficult, but if you get it working it's a real winner.

Language: drawing in the audience

The words you write need to translate into natural and comfortable sounds. As I said earlier, when you're delivering your speech you have to sound as if you're not reading from a script at all.

Don't forget, most people at the wedding will know you well enough to be familiar with your style of speaking. The human voice has a variety of qualities, making each one distinctive. You may have heard of security devices that can tell the identity of a person based on their 'voiceprint'. Just like a fingerprint, each of us has a different voice – deep or high, singsong or flat, gravelly or smooth. On top of that we have our own unique way of phrasing our words.

When writing your speech don't try to hide your personality – be yourself! This will make writing your speech script a thousand times easier than writing a formal speech. If your speech is formal, you won't connect with the audience. That connection is crucial to how your words are received (their effect) and how you handle yourself throughout the speech (e.g. nerves).

To give you a better, more in-depth understanding of this we'll look at the main elements of language you need to be aware of in a speech including:

- Formal vs natural voice
- Pace
- Rhythm
- Flow
- Crafting words using images and symbolism.

Formal versus natural voice

Ask most people to write a few words to say in public and they may write what is called text. A 'text' is written to be read, not said. It's formal and generally obeys grammatical rules. To give you an idea, read this aloud: 'A wedding day is not only a ceremony. A wedding day is a celebration.'

Great at school, not in a speech to loved ones. So, what you'll be writing is a 'script'. The same text would sound much better like this (read it aloud): 'A wedding day isn't just a ceremony – it's a celebration.'

The script will capture your normal manner of speaking and people will warm to your words more. You'll also find it much easier to rehearse your speech when its language is your language.

Pace

Although the words will be written in the same way as you speak, you must still alter them to give the audience a chance to absorb certain points and to become involved in your story. Your speech is not simply a task of uttering words – it's sharing wishes, feelings and memories with the wedding party and guests. Just imagine you are in the audience listening to your speech (this technique is discussed further on). Does it draw you in? Does it interest you? The best speeches inform and involve the audience.

Write your sentences to match your voice and your breathing pattern. Go over the speech and see where you need to pause to allow the audience to absorb a point or draw them into one. Pauses are also very effective in the gap between a question you ask, and the answer you give.

Example

'When [BRIDE] and [GROOM] told us they were going to get married I thought ahead and wondered how I'd feel on the wedding day. [PAUSE] Is our little girl leaving us? Will she stop helping me with my tax returns? Will we still be father and daughter? [PAUSE] Well, when she placed her arm in mine today all I could feel was immense pride and complete love for our little girl, for this beautiful woman ... our daughter and now also [GROOM'S] wonderful wife.'

Rhythm

Another technique to help draw in the audience is rhythm. This is the use and placement of certain words to create a natural feeling of rhythm. If you've read or heard poetry or fiction, then you'll have encountered rhythm. There are two very effective types of rhythm you can use: alliteration and parallel sentences.

Alliteration is the recurrence of sounds (and syllables). This is normally done with the beginning of words. For example, 'May you always have love and laughter in your life.'

The alliteration here was the recurrence of the letter 'l' in 'love', 'laughter' and 'life'. This technique adds lyrical rhythm to such a simple phrase. Use it sparingly, and most of all, use it where it counts. The above example was used to express the speaker's wishes for the married couple.

You'll also find alliteration works best in a series of three (as in the above example). Don't get carried away with it or you may find yourself getting tongue-tied.

Parallel sentences can be used to stress a point or a series of points. For example, 'Love makes the impossible possible ... Love warms us on cold days ... Love gives us something to live for ... Love is pure ... Love is what I see tonight between [BRIDE] and [GROOM].'

As you can see, parallel sentences used in this way allow you to put something such as the love between people in a grander context. It also allows you to phrase what you want to say in a neat and clear manner.

Flow

Flow is ensuring a smooth connection from one point to another. If you've ever tried explaining to a person how to do a certain task you would have used flow: 'You close the door. *Then* you turn the dial all the way to the right.'

Then was used to keep the flow and clarify the next point.

In a speech, it's not too hard to write a couple of sentences to cover a certain point. However, most people find it difficult to keep the flow of their speech going. You can also create flow through a rhetorical question:

Example

'What kept me going despite all this? [PAUSE] [BRIDE]. She never let me give up on myself.'

Using the word 'meanwhile' is another way of bridging two connected points:

Example

'I spent weeks wondering if [BRIDE] was even remotely interested in me. I didn't want to look a fool and ask, but I didn't want to lose her either ... meanwhile, it turns out she was asking my friends if I was interested in her!'

It may seem obvious, but many people neglect the flow of their speech. It's a valuable way of keeping the audience's attention and there are many words and phrases you can use to improve the flow, including *however, anyway, anyhow, at the same time*.

You'll find the ones which work for you when you start re-reading your script out loud. That's also when you'll spot where there are problems with flow in the first place. How? Well, whenever a piece in your speech seems disjointed or too sudden or out of place – that's a flow problem. Try different ways of saying it aloud and connecting to the next point.

Crafting words: using images and symbolism

To add life to words in your speech, try out techniques used by writers (especially fiction writers). These are especially effective when used in any stories or anecdotes you may be including.

Example

'One bright January morning, I sprung the idea on [BRIDE] to take a drive into the country ... to see where the road took us. Of course, I already had a place in mind – a small sparkling lake surrounded by grassy rolling hills. [PAUSE] It was there we stopped. We walked down to the edge of the water. After a moment, I knelt on one knee, looked up at her and asked if she'd be my wife.'

Now, although that stretched the length out somewhat, it's worth it for such an important part of the speech. Of course, you need to watch the quantity, but don't concentrate on that at the cost of quality. On the other hand, it sometimes takes fewer words to better describe an image. Instead of saying, 'She looked at me and started smiling and crying and nodding.' Try saying, 'Her eyes gave me her answer.'

Figurative language is another way of describing something in a more interesting way – similes and metaphors give language an extra angle. A simile is where you compare one thing to another. The two are usually linked by using 'as' or 'like'. For example, 'As happy as a cat that's got the cream.' So, instead of, 'We laughed all evening.' Try, 'We laughed *like lunatics* all evening.'

A metaphor is different – it transforms one thing to another.

Example

'I knew [BRIDE] was planning a trip even though she denied it. My suspicions were confirmed two days later when I opened the broom cupboard and was attacked by flocks of travel brochures, tumbling out of their hidden nest.'

So, where you can, or where the speech demands it, spice it up a little. Don't get too carried away and use it too liberally, just use it here or there. Try to get the audience to visualize what you're describing as this will make your story richer and draw them in.

Using humour

Humour is a great way to break the ice and open a speech. There is nothing better than hearing people laugh to make you – and them – relax. A wedding is a celebration after all and opening with humour is the best technique for relaxing people and encouraging them to enjoy the event. It could be a joke or a witty anecdote. However, humour in a wedding speech must also be used carefully.

A witty anecdote (which you may have identified in the planning stage earlier) is always a welcome inclusion in a wedding speech. It could be a funny story about either the bride or groom. Maybe about when they were a child. Perhaps in the lead-up to the wedding day there was a hitch in the arrangements, a story which now, in the safety of the past, is worth telling. Whatever you choose, just be sure it won't cause offence and doesn't require a laborious explanation. Remember: the hook has to catch the audience.

The same goes for straightforward jokes. There is a very fine line between having them rolling in the aisles and having them rolling their eyes in polite pain. Remember: you are writing for the audience.

The saying goes in comedy: if in doubt, leave it out. The general rules for jokes or humour are:

- Are you comfortable enough to be able to relate the joke properly?
- Will the joke be well received and understood by nearly all of the audience? The guests could range from toddlers to a centenarian.

- Leave private jokes out unless you can explain them properly to the rest of the audience. Family or groups of friends may have a standing joke – that's fine, but will it be lost on the rest of the audience?
- Obviously, sexist, racist, ageist or any form of minority jokes may result in hurt feelings (theirs or yours) so avoid them at all costs.
- The same applies to dirty jokes or risqué comments – risqué is generally fine, but only up to a point.
- Steer clear of making harsh jokes about the married couple – especially the bride. If you are absolutely positive they won't be offended make sure you close up the joke with serious praise (but, watch this one – it has gone wrong at many a wedding).

Using props

Props or other stage equipment (but please be sensible about this) are a great way of enhancing a joke or funny story. They are also a handy technique for making the other guests feel included.

Props can be used as physical gags in themselves (for example, a book presented as marital advice such as *War and Peace* or *Cooking for Dummies*). Props are also useful for illustrating a funny story. For example, while recalling what the groom was like as a child you might have some of his toys to hand (teddy bear, toy car or action figure). You could embellish on the truth and announce his mother gave you some of his childhood toys to show at the reception and then produce a Barbie doll!

Another gag is to read from a fake letter supposedly written by either the bride or groom as a child. It could be about anything – embarrassing things he or she liked doing as a child or what that person wanted to be when he or she grew up – whatever you think the guests might find believable or amusing. Of course, if it's not obvious don't tell them it's a fake until the end (or maybe not at all – keep them guessing).

Closing the speech

What impression would you like to leave the audience with at the end of your speech? Whatever it is, that will guide you for your closing lines. Similar to the opening lines, it could be humorous or sentimental.

Your speech should flow to a neat close and not leave the audience hanging in the air. Depending on your role on the day, once your core speech has ended the only item left will be your toast proposal. For examples of what you should include in your toast, refer to the sample speeches.

Transferring from a script to a cue card

The idea of a cue card is to summarize the main topics of your speech in point form and in sequence.

When you finalize your speech in full script form (i.e. word for word) you'll have to practise it. Don't panic – you won't believe how easy it actually is to get your script practised enough to allow you to read from a cue card on the night.

For a cue card you can use standard-sized index cards, which you'll find in most stationery shops. Otherwise, you can simply use a sheet of paper.

To transfer your completed script to a cue card, review the script and write down its main topics in short, single lines. Write it out roughly until you're happy that each line captures what you want to say on each topic. These 'one-liner' points can even be the first sentence of each topic – use whatever jogs your memory the best.

Later, when you are practising, you may find that some topics in your speech need prompting on the cue card more than others, so adjust the cue card to match.

Cue card example

Write out the words in large clear capital letters, making the card easier to read. The example below is short, but you can put more on your cards, if it helps. You may find you want to note down some specific phrases, quotations or details. Just remember to keep the lines short and write out only enough to prompt your memory.

By the time you've practised your speech enough, the cue card will only serve as a prompt. Some people find they don't use it in the end, but it helps to create one in the first place.

Here's a short example of a father of the bride's cue card:

1   BEFORE I START, I'D LIKE TO THANK:
    • [GROOM'S] PARENTS FOR THEIR HELP
    • GUESTS FOR COMING
2   QUOTE FROM POEM
3   STORY: DAY [BRIDE] BROUGHT [GROOM] HOME
4   WISHES FOR THEIR FUTURE
5   TOAST TO BRIDE AND GROOM

Delivering your speech

You've completed your speech script and transferred it to cue cards. Your speech is ready – the only thing left is to do is to prepare yourself.

This section will guide you through techniques to use your voice effectively, learn how to hold your posture correctly, cope with any nerves and deliver your speech successfully.

Using your voice effectively

The way you utilize your voice in normal everyday conversation is very different from the way you use it to address a gathering of people. In public speaking, you are using your voice to paint a picture in the minds of the audience.

Remember: the rule of a good speech is to get the audience's attention, say what you want to say and leave them feeling uplifted and happy.

Try to make your tone of voice and choice of words interesting. Think how you would describe a walk through a forest to someone without sight – the words you use and emphasis would change dramatically.

Also, your words will need to be heard clearly. People won't hear you if you speak too fast, too quietly or squeeze the entire speech into one tense breath. So, how do you ensure your words will be heard – and clearly? In this chapter, you'll learn how to improve your public speaking by:

- Assessing your voice.
- Emphasizing and clearly pronouncing words.
- Pacing your words.
- Projecting your voice.

Assess your voice

First of all, you need to find out what elements of your public speaking voice will need attention, so, it's a good idea if you take a little time to assess your voice. Use a recording device for this or ask someone to listen to you read your speech. Have that person sit away from you, preferably in a large room.

Read your speech aloud and record it. Give it a couple of tries if you like. When you're finished, play it back and see how clearly you've spoken. Try to listen to it as if you are a guest. Your speech should be clear to everybody at the reception. This is what you are listening out for:

- Did you sound too flat or monotonous and as if you were concentrating too much?
- Did you make good use of pauses to add expectation or let a point sink in?
- Did you emphasize certain phrases or words sufficiently in order to hammer home a particular point?
- Did you speak too fast or too slowly?
- Did you speak clearly enough to identify every word?
- Are you conveying the message you want to?

Voice tone and pitch

When you're comfortable and speaking in normal conversation, the tone of your voice will vary depending on your subject, your audience and whether your tone is light-hearted or serious. The pitch of your voice also changes to match these criteria. However, when it comes to public speaking, people tend to be distracted by their nervousness and as a result they end up speaking in a monotone and raising the pitch of their voice.

There is no perfect tone or pitch in speech delivery. The perfect tone and pitch are those which best suit your own voice and the speech you are giving. Listen to the recording of your speech and identify where you could alter the tone and pitch to emphasize certain areas.

It's important to keep the audience listening. This can be achieved through changing your emphasis in tone and pitch. Newsreaders on TV and radio use such changes to capture and hold your attention.

Speaking of news, the good news is that the more you practise your speech before the wedding, the better you will know the right tone and pitch to use. As you learn and become comfortable with the words, you'll have to concentrate less. And, as with normal conversation, your words will sound far more natural.

Emphasizing with words – and without

With words

Listening to your speech played back, you may already have spotted when some words require more emphasis than others.

For example, instead of, '... that's when I knew she was serious', add emphasis to the most important word in the sentence – the one at the heart of what you're trying to say in any particular sentence or paragraph.

So, in the above example you could place stress on the word '*knew*', '... that's when I *knew* she was serious.'

Not only does this technique emphasize certain core elements of your speech, it also guides guests and keeps their attention.

Without words

Although pauses were discussed earlier (see page 70), now that you are polishing the sound of the speech and are increasingly familiar with your written words, you may spot areas of your speech that require a better placing of pauses. This may be because a certain point needs to be allowed to sink in. This is especially effective in serious and poignant parts of a speech – a well-placed pause adds to the feeling of importance and sincerity.

Pauses also create a gap between one point and the next. If you're telling a funny story or a joke, a pause will create that air of anticipation required to deliver a punchline. If you are changing from one subject to another (and therefore changing from one tone to another) a pause will allow you to do this without causing confusion.

Don't overuse pauses or your speech may end up with too many gaps and silences, but if there is a pause (comma, full stop or your own inserted [PAUSE]) in your speech then obey it. If you don't, you might confuse or lose the audience (or yourself). Remember: if you have a pause between a touching or sentimental subject and a new or up-beat subject, make sure you invigorate the audience as you move out of the pause by using the most fitting tone to best match each section of the speech. It's a ride – take them on it.

Getting the point across clearly

Beyond your voice's tone and pitch, your words need to be heard clearly. Other than how loud or soft you need to speak (discussed later), you need to make sure you're not speaking too fast and that your words are coming across clearly.

Pace (or speed)

Listen to your recording. Are you rushing through your words? Be wary of this, especially on the day as nerves can cause people to race through their speech. (It's almost as if they want to get the whole thing over with as quickly as possible!)

It may seem appealing to rush, but don't do it. If you rush, you're more likely to make a mistake. Also, guests will not be given the chance to absorb key points – in the end, you'll have finished your speech in record time, but no-one will have really got into it.

So, set the pace of your speech to suit your style. On the day, your breathing will probably be faster (due to some nerves). If you can, practise your speech at a pace that comes naturally to you, which should also help lessen any nerves on the day.

By that stage you should find the pace occurs far more naturally (via repetition).

Of course, this doesn't mean you need to ... speak ... too ... slowly. Make sure the pace doesn't slow down to the stage where people are falling asleep.

Articulation

While your speech is designed to sound natural when spoken in your natural voice, you need to make sure that each word can be clearly understood. Stage actors, like public speakers, achieve this through articulation and projection.

Projecting your voice: microphone or no microphone?

Do you know if the reception will have a microphone? Whether or not there is one affects how you project your voice.

With a microphone

The important thing to remember about microphones is that their sensitivity varies. Different PA (public address) systems and different locations produce different qualities of sound. On top of that, people sometimes find it difficult to gauge how loud or soft they should speak with a microphone. When we're up there, we mainly tend to hear the sound from our own mouth and not the PA system.

As a general rule, don't have the microphone too close to your mouth. This overloads the output, making it difficult for guests to discern your words clearly (many of you will have heard this effect before). It's a good idea to discuss any concerns about the microphone with the venue beforehand. The staff may be familiar with the sound quality and levels.

However, if all else fails you can always adjust your voice when you stand up. At the beginning of your speech, look towards the back of the room – are people straining to hear you? You may need to raise the level of your voice a little but you won't need to raise it too dramatically or shout. Remember to speak at a slow and steady pace, clearly pronouncing your words.

Just remember to relax before you first speak – take in a few slow, easy, steady breaths as you prepare yourself (more on preparation later).

Without a microphone

Articulation and projection really come into play if there is no microphone at the venue. Exaggerate your lip movements when pronouncing words. Speak firmly and confidently. One side effect of forcing yourself to 'speak to be heard' is it boosts your confidence. They say fear feeds itself – well, confidence also feeds itself. If you make yourself sound confident, you'll begin to feel more confident.

The very best way of ensuring you'll be heard by everyone is to use another theatrical technique. Pretend you are speaking directly to those furthest away from you. Your voice should be loud and clear enough to be heard by the people at the back of the room. Again, don't raise your voice to the point of shouting.

Body language: posture and gesture

The way you hold your body in public speaking and the use of body language make a difference to the quality of your speech.

Posture

When a person is nervous, they tend to stand with their shoulders curled in and their head down. This conveys the wrong message to the audience and restricts your ability to speak confidently and well. Nerves also cause a speaker's airway to tighten and this can badly affect our confidence and voice control.

No-one expects you to be a rousing orator – everyone expects and understands some degree of nervousness. However, if a speaker is hunched up with nerves, the audience will sense this and be drawn away from your words. This goes against a speaker's most important task – to draw in the crowd. There is a way round this.

What to do

To project a confident image remember to keep your:

- Head upright.
- Shoulders relaxed.
- Back straight.
- Chest out.

Also, place your feet firmly on the ground about shoulder width apart. In addition to projecting confident body language, this also frees up your air passage so you will be able to control and project your voice far better. People will react positively and as a result, you will too. So (literally), chin up!

What not to do

Body language is a funny thing. Often the way we hold ourselves can be misconstrued by those around us. When you're giving your speech:

- Don't lean on the table – it conveys aggression while also making you tense up.
- Don't dig your hands into your pockets – again it will cause you to hunch and tense up and your hands will get sweaty, possibly triggering more nerves.
- Don't tense your legs – every now and then subtly shift your weight from one leg to the other (but don't get carried away and look as if you need to dash to the toilet).
- Don't fold your arms in front of you – it gives the impression of defensiveness.

Remember: you want to draw the audience in with your happiness and friendliness.

Gesture

Gestures are the non-verbal words in your speech. Similar to a speaker's posture, there are some 'dos and don'ts'.

What to do

Use gestures to enhance certain elements of your speech. Gestures can be:

- Hand movements.
- Facial expressions.
- Eye contact.
- Head movements.

Some people are known to talk with their hands. It's a very expressive method for conveying a story. Nerves have a habit of restricting hand movement, but once you start moving as you normally would in conversation, you'll find you relax more (your body will feel as though it's on familiar territory).

Facial expressions are another natural communicator of feelings and ideas. Again, the more you allow your body to speak as it does in normal conversation, the more you'll relax. And what's one of the best facial expressions to use? Your natural smile.

Eye contact is another important element. Don't fix your eyes for too long on one person or thing. Think of a fly-fisher constantly casting a bait onto the water. You can keep the audience's attention by regularly casting a glance at different parts of the room (along with moving your body). Of course, don't do this too much or you'll get dizzy.

If something in your speech could do with a head movement, such as a puzzled tilt to the side, use it. This physical action not only enhances what you've just said, it acts as a trigger to the audience (again, drawing them in).

Finally, to feel comfortable with your gestures for the day, include them with your speech practice. Do this in front of a long mirror or a video camera.

What not to do

Some people worry that when they're making their speech the audience will be watching their every move for a flaw. This isn't the case. Ask yourself, have you deliberately done this? No, most likely not. However, people will be aware if you get carried away and make too many forced gestures. So:

- Don't add so many gestures that they become a distraction (both for yourself and your audience).
- Don't clasp your hands together as you speak – you may begin tensing them which will then make you feel tense.

- Don't wag your finger or raise a clenched fist unless it's obviously humorous.
- Don't allow your hands to fidget with your speech card, watch or shirt collar (it's an obvious sign of nerves).
- Don't lift your hand in front of your mouth as it will block the sound.
- Don't try to force your smile – if you're nervous or your smile muscles have had a work-out all day – it could make you look like you are grimacing.

Coping with nerves

Now that you have those public speaking techniques under your belt and have begun practising your speech, you're already well prepared to cope with nerves on the night. Again, just like learning to ride a bicycle, once you have the basic training, the fear is already greatly reduced.

I say greatly reduced, because practically anyone delivering a speech in public gets nervous (before and during). It's completely natural. Nerves only become a problem in a speech if you're not confident reading your material or you don't calm yourself properly beforehand.

With the techniques you've learned so far and by practising your speech, the first cause is dealt with. In this chapter you'll learn to manage your nerves as well as how to deal with speech speed bumps such as mistakes and interruptions.

Believe it or not, the guests sitting out there are on your side. This is not a job interview or a courtroom plea for mercy. This is you speaking to people who, just like yourself, are celebrating a special occasion. Think positively about your speech and remind yourself that it's going to be just fine.

Before the speech

Whatever you do, don't drink to calm your nerves before the speech! If someone suggests you get a drink down you for that reason, say "no". It may seem like a good idea (especially if you've already had a couple) but it is a huge no-no. Your concentration will go out of the window, so stay sober. Of course, once your speech is finished have a drink – you deserve it!

Before you stand up to speak, try this relaxation technique:

- Sit with your arms by your sides and feet firmly on the ground.
- Take in a big deep breath through your nose as you clench your fists, press your feet into the floor and hunch up your shoulders.
- Hold it for a couple of seconds then slowly exhale, at the same time slowly loosening your fists, shoulders and feet – let your stresses fall and float away as you exhale completely.

As you stand up, breathe easily. If you feel your chest tensing, take in a slow, deep breath and relax it as you exhale. Then make sure you assume a good posture (see pages 86–87). Before speaking, slowly and calmly look around the room as you would when meeting up with friends. Give the crowd a welcoming smile.

During the speech

- If your mouth starts to go dry, take a sip of water. If there isn't any nearby, use an old trick of imagining you are sucking a juicy orange or an ice lolly.
- If there are any interruptions such as a fork falling onto the floor or a chair being moved, ignore it. These are normal sounds during any wedding speech.
- If you hear some people talking or whispering in the room, don't let it get to you. If someone is talking during a speech that's simply their poor manners – concentrate on your words.
- If you make a joke and no-one really laughs, don't try to rescue it or start again. Move on or make a joke out of it with a comment such as, 'I thought it was a poor joke too.'
- If someone starts heckling you (in good humour) pause right there. Let them throw a quick line (it is usually funny

anyway). You can always use the reply, 'I thought the point of heckling was to make the speaker look like an idiot, not the heckler.'

- If you get lost in your words, don't panic. Just cover up with a cough and refer to your cue card again. What was the last part you said? Just like finding keys, think about when you came in the door, where did you put them?

Final words of advice

There are three final rules you need to know in order to deliver a great speech: practice, practice, practice! Overkill? Not at all. If you know your material, the rest spreads like soft butter on warm toast.

To check on your speaking voice, practise and ask someone to listen to your speech. Also record and play it back to listen for any flaws (don't be afraid to change words in your speech script). To check on your gestures and posture, practise in front of a long mirror or even film yourself.

Practise as regularly as you can. What you are aiming for is to know the speech almost off the top of your head. Don't forget, you need to practise the final script of the speech so that you can simply rely on the cue card on the night.

Finally, good luck with your speech.

Everyone is capable of more than they believe.

So, stand up, say your piece and enjoy the moment!

Useful resources

Websites

Useful Information

www.useful-information.info/quotations/wedding_quotes.html

The Quote Garden

www.quotegarden.com/weddings.html

Famous Quotes & Quotations

www.famous-quotes-and-quotations.com/wedding-quotes.html

The Bestman's Speech

www.thebestmanspeech.com

Books

P. Agnew, *Heartsongs: Readings for Weddings*, Rider & Co, 2006

Wedding Readings, Poems and Vows (Confetti), Hamlyn, 2007

A. Vasudevan (ed.), *Poems and Readings for Weddings and Civil Partnerships*, New Holland, 2009

J. Watson, *Poems and Readings for Weddings*, Penguin, 2004

Index

Notes